Sherice Lanae Nixon

Worth the Wait

Poems to encourage

Young ladies in abstinence

until marriage

Sherice Lanae Nixon

ISBN-13: 978-1537223025

ISBN-10: 153722302X

Unless otherwise noted, Scripture taken from *The Message*. Copyright © 1993, 1994, 1995, 1996, 2000, 2001, 2002

DEDICATION

This book is dedicated to my late Grandparents King Richard Nixon,

"Daddy King" and Shirley Margaret Rose Fitzgerald Nixon aka "Grammy"

whose marriage was a model to my young mind as I grew up. It is also dedicated

to the late Cassandra Thornton, a woman who lived her life holy before God as a

single woman serving in prayer, giving and fasting until she met her ultimate

Love, face to face in eternity. Thank you, Cassandra, for speaking into my life

and encouraging me to write this book.

ACKNOWLEDGMENTS

To Father God, who has shown me what true love is, to my mother, Rose Nixon-Thomas, for your constant prayers, encouragement and humor; to my family for your continued support and to my friends who make life more enjoyable- thank you! Thank you to my late father, Wendell Davis. Your kindness, love and creativity were truly handed down to me. To every pastor, leader, and servant of the Lord who has imparted into my life throughout the years, thank you! Special thanks to Jesus People Ministries Church, World Harvest Church, Baruch Christian Fellowship and Kingdom Life & Dominion Church. The impartations that I have received throughout the years have helped me to become the woman that I am today and that I will continue to grow into. To my best friend and husband to be, thank you for encouraging me to be who it is that God says I am!

PREFACE

In today's culture there is so much pressure to be in wrong

relationships. Television sitcoms show women striving to gain the attention

and affections of men even to the point of participating in ungodly and

adulterous lifestyles in an attempt to gain love or something that looks like

it. God has called His people to a higher standard and dimension of living

especially in regards to relationships. According to Scripture God's design

is for one man and one woman to be together for a lifetime. This collection

of poems and songs is designed to encourage young women who desire to live

life by God's design for marriage as they await their "knight in shining

armor". These poems and songs are pieces of my heart throughout the

years. They have encouraged and strengthened me and they will encourage

and strengthen you too. As you read these poems- laugh with me, cry with

me, ponder with me and allow the Lord to encourage your heart. As you

wait for your future husband know that your relationship with the

ultimate Husband-man, God, is growing stronger, and that He is making

you into a stronger woman (spiritually, mentally, physically, financially,

Sherice Lanae Nixon

etc.). He is preparing you to be a better wife to your future husband, and he is preparing your future husband to be the best mate for you. As you allow God to be your focus, your reason and first love, realize that one day you will see that it was all Worth the Wait.

CONTENTS

The Songs

The Poems

Worth the Wait

<u>Wait</u>

"So don't try to get out of anything prematurely. Let it do its work so you become mature and well-developed, not deficient in any way. If you don't know what you're doing, pray to the Father. He loves to help. You'll get his help, and won't be condescended to when you ask for it." James 1:4-5

Wait so you can escape the baby mama drama, the trauma and the heartache

Wait so you can bypass the pain, the shame, the blame, and the mind games

Wait until you are sure and not have to endure, the impure, and the insecure

Wait until you know your price, it's pretty nice, it cost another man his entire life

Wait so you can obtain the wealth, good health, a better self and more on your shelf

Wait until you've done everything that you knew that you should

Wait even though sometimes you may be ridiculed, made fun of, mocked and misunderstood

Wait 'cause so many others are following your example

Wait to show the mockers that they were never ever going to get a sample

Wait 'cause God is forming you more and more into His image

Wait... this will be the testimony you will give to your children's children

Wait because you know this is what God requires no matter how long the time

Wait as you blossom in your style, your desires and find your peace of mind

Wait until you know whose you are, who you are and what you are all about

Wait until you meet the one that agrees with you so that when you get hooked up you don't have to be dragged out!

Wait....

Wait I say on the Lord!

Have you acknowledged the benefits of waiting until marriage for sex?

Confession

*"Words kill, words give life;
they're either poison or fruit—you choose" Proverbs 18:21*

I am a mighty woman of God called for this hour

I am filled with the love of God-I am filled with His power

I operate in Kingdom wisdom and authority

Delegated to me by Christ Himself the King of Kings

I have no fear because He lives within me-He's Christ in me,

the hope of glory

The Holy Spirit is my very best Friend and Guide

Giving me comfort and counsel

Teaching me the Word and how to live the Godly life

I am never defeated I am always on top

When the enemy tries to rise up against me

The God in me tells him He has got to stop!

Cause the earth is the Lord's and everything in it

Daily I am walking in the dominion that I have been given

Humbly, I so decree I so declare and I so establish

Because Lord you said as I speak and believe...I shall have it

3

*Have you fully grasped the reality of how making confessions
over your life affects you on a daily basis?*

Single Time, a Defining Time

"I want you to live as free of complications as possible.
When you're unmarried, you're free to concentrate
on simply pleasing the Master." I Corinthians 7:32

Single time is truly a defining time

God shapes, forms and He builds

He strengthens affirms and gives

Peeling, carving, breaking

While at the same time- Restoring, filling and making

Making me into all that He desired and ordained me to be

The perfected, matured me-the directed submitted me

The connected, obedient me- He sees me

The one He knew before there was time, seasons, night or day

The one who loves Him-With all that is within

The one who rejoices-At the sound of His voice and follows

His commands and ways

The one who forever sings His songs of praise and

Even in the midst of an evil generation will still walk out his

Holy ways

The one who longs after righteousness and peace

And loves my neighbor and others the way that I love me......

For before I was formed in my mother's womb, by Him I was

already known

and every single day of my life is in His hands

My life has never ever been my own.

So I give it to Him

Wholly, Holy, Solely, Willingly

Truly....this single time is a defining time. and...I will... bless

Him...in every single moment, in every single hour, every

single minute and every single second because He defines me

and He reminds me-time and time again

Who I am both in and out of time- I am His child

There is beauty is singleness, can you see it?

Wait for the Great

"So let's not allow ourselves to get fatigued doing good. At the right time we will harvest a good crop if we don't give up, or quit." Galatians 6:9

It's better to wait for the great than to decide on the wrong guy

'Cause this is for life, you know, in the good and in the not so good

In the laughter and in the cry

Ask yourself,

Is his character strong so that when the storms of life rage you know that he's going to hold on?

Is your respect for him so high that his ego you won't even try?

Now, if you just want a body then anybody will do

But if you say that you want the very best

Wait on the goodness that God has for you

It's better to wait for the great than to decide on Mr. OK.

Does his vision find rest in your heart of hearts? Can you stand by him in his God given call?

You know that two can't walk together except they be agreed

If you're not joined together by God and His purpose

We both know that relationship will struggle to last long so don't stall!

Come on, wait for the Great, don't you dare settle for second best

It's God's will to bless you with nothing less

You two should be singing in the same key

Perhaps two different notes but creating a beautiful harmony

The Lord Himself should be the song and the melody

A threefold chord in perfect unity

My sister, wait for the Great, I say, don't compromise with an imposter

Just so you can have a name on the roster

'Cause when you unite this thing is for life

This is not a joke

Be equally yoked

Saved, sanctified, filled with God's Spirit

Money in the bank but humility every minute

Disciplined, focused, with character and strength

Make sure he's loving, kind, a family man

Save yourself the tears and wasted years

By inclining your ear to heaven and hearing, listening to

When you have met an eligible Bachelor, Mr. Right for you

Not Mr. Right Now, Not Mr. Right Away,

But the right timing, season and the very answer to what you've prayed.

Not perfect, but being perfected-moving in God's direction

Not sinless but sinning less-pursuing and honoring God with intention

Yes, the man that God has for you will be great but you just got to wait

GREAT

Good, Righteous, Encouraging, Anointed, Trustworthy

Who wants to wait for years only to choose unwisely due to impatience?

The Master Builder

"For every house is built by someone, but God is the builder of everything. "Moses was faithful as a servant in all God's house," bearing witness to what would be spoken by God in the future. ⁶ But Christ is faithful as the Son over God's house. And we are his house, if indeed we hold firmly to our confidence and the hope in which we glory." Hebrews 3:4-6 NIV

The longer it takes to make a foundation, the higher the building will be.

Don't get frustrated while you wait 'because you don't know the depths of what your marriage will be

To have and to hold when nights get cold

To forgive and to forget so together you both will mold

Life is preparing you- getting you ready for when this next part of your life unfolds

Layer by layer revelation will come

Of who you are in Me, then one day, who you both are as one

So be patient my child as I make you better and better

A better you alone today, creates a better you on that day (tomorrow) together

No other foundation can be made

except one built on Me, you see

And no house will truly stand unless it's built on the Solid Rock, and that's Me

And no Architectural structure that I am building

11

will fully stay intact

Unless it's exactly the way that I want it to be

From bottom to top and from front to back

The longer it takes to build the foundation the higher
the building will be

Grant Me the time My child to make a more beautiful he

And a more beautiful she

And when you two finally meet and connect

what a joy it will be!

Because it will not only bring you both great joy, it will bring
great pleasure to ME

Just remember this ....

I make everything beautiful in My time

I am the Master Builder, the original blue print is in My hand –
your being here, your life- it was not your decision-it came
from My mind

And as you trust Me with your whole heart and allow Me to
complete My design

You will see that all that you endured was intentional but not
allowed for your demise

Because in the end all will say, "This is the Lord's doing and it
is marvelous in our eyes"

I am the Master Builder, the One who said "pray and believe"

Is it not My word that says that "if you give then you shall
receive?"

Don't you know that I give the best gifts: a husband, a family,
is that all you are asking for? Is that it?

I gave my only begotten Son for you how much more will I
give you this wish?

I said, the man that endures temptations will receive the crown
of life

I am the one who said that it was not good for man to be alone
and chose to create for him a "wife"

I am causing your faith to arise and grow

To praise and worship and seek me no matter how long

And when you don't understand continue to sow

Until you are no longer moved by dates and times

Because you have heard my word

and you just "know that you know".

Yes, I am building you more and more for

What I want you both to be

Don't pay attention to how long it's taking

My child, pay attention to me!

I have the Master Plan

I said, the Blue Print is in My Hand

And if you could discern keenly

You would see that I have been working speedily

So surrender the anxious thoughts and rest in the truth

That before you even asked I have already answered you

Trust that I am working in the background and making all

things good
And before you know it,
You won't be there in solitude
There will be two of you.

Why is there a time difference in the construction of a home verses a skyscraper building?

Alone and Not Lonely

"...Don't be obsessed with getting more material things. Be relaxed with what you have. Since God assured us, "I'll never let you down, never walk off and leave you," we can boldly quote, God is there, ready to help; I'm fearless no matter what. Who or what can get to me?" " Hebrews 13:5-6

I am alone but I am never lonely

In my heart of hearts your word is deep inside me

The Alpha and the Omega

The one who was and is and is to come

Within this heart of mine live the Father, the Holy Spirit and the Son

How could I ever be alone when angels are encamped all around?

They begin to move and rearrange things every time I praise, lift my hands and shout

I can't worry about who is here or who is not here with me

Cause every time I turn around

Your goodness and mercy are following me

And every nation calls me blessed- for this and more my King, I offer you my best

All of my heart

You called me alone and if You so choose, You will add

But You are not limited to adding anyone

You are greater than any man

And if I have to walk another mile alone then so let it be

I will take comfort knowing that You, my God,

are here with me

'Cause me plus God is always a majority

I can gently hear the voice of the Holy Spirit speaking to me

Telling me good things about how He loves me and wants to prosper me

As I rehearse His words my heart grows full of peace

Now I can face the world.

Now I can accomplish anything.

Knowing I am never really alone,

God is right here with me.

I may be alone, but I am certainly not lonely

Have you truly grasped the fact that God is always here with you?

What if?

"I've learned by now to be quite content whatever my circumstances. I'm just as happy with little as with much, with much as with little. I've found the recipe for being happy whether full or hungry, hands full or hands empty. Whatever I have, wherever I am, I can make it through anything in the One who makes me who I am." Philippians 4:11b-13

What if you never get married and share your heart with another?

What if you are never granted the earthly friend, confidant and lover?

What if your days are spent in sacrifice and service to the world,

Never having a family of your own yet mentoring many boys and girls?

What if you lived on the mission field all of your days,

From land to land- sea to sea- spreading the Good News and declaring God's praise,

And your desires for the luxuries of this world seem to be erased?

Would you feel like your life was wasted and not well spent?

Or would you appreciate the fact that you were heaven sent?

Sent from glory to help heal the lost and the dying

Sent from eternity from the Father to comfort the broken, the lost, the hurting; those who are crying.

And what if you get married

and are blessed with a family so great

And serve your spouse with love and honor, rising early and staying up late

And together you display the beauty of a threefold Chord

Your spouse and you sold out to the Lord?

What if your union's daily actions exemplify His love to all,

And together you serve the Lord encouraging each other to fulfill God's call?

Your greatness plus your spouse's greatness will be double success

One can chase a thousand and two ten thousand so you know the rest.

Together you can serve on the mission field of God's choice

And there will be power in agreement as you both pray unto the Lord with one voice

And a righteous seed before the Lord you both will bear

Training and teaching them in the admonition and the fear

Of the Lord with great care

And on that great day the Lord will say "Well done my child, enter into my rest"

To both the one who was married and to the one whom He kept

*Will you serve God with your whole heart regardless of what
the future holds for you concerning marriage?*

God's son, but Not the One

"Don't be harsh or impatient with an older man. Talk to him as you would your own father, and to the younger men as your brothers. Reverently honor an older woman as you would your mother and the younger women as sisters".

I Timothy 5:1-2

He is not your husband but be careful how you treat him

He may not be your cup of tea,

but someone else in this world will need him

He is your brother, even your brother in Christ

Just as you have been born again, he too has experienced new life

Do you know how much courage it took for him to come and talk to you?

He may have prayed and waited for months before even trying to step to you

Now you're cutting him off with your abrasive speech

But I thought you were Virtuous...

pouring out grace whenever you speak

Let's not insult our brothers who give us compliments

After all, who else should they attempt to pursue, aren't you claiming you're the Proverbs 31 woman?

Don't let the women of the world treat men with more respect

Being virtuous is about the way we live our lives and treat others not just how we dress

Modesty and beauty first start with our hearts, spirit and soul

We should take it as an encouragement knowing that you are
already complete and whole

And if any man is drawn to you, attracted by your essence

Make sure they leave encouraged and strengthened in God
when they leave your very presence

And if your heart has been broken and you've experienced pain

Don't blame it on another man and relive the pain again and
again

Let the Lord heal each and every wound

And receive with love the people that God allows to cross
paths with you

Yes, it's true he may not be what you are looking for

But do you realize that maybe he too has been broken and
seeking the Lord to restore

And since you are a woman of Virtue then you should pour

Life and vitality forth to him, lead him to Christ, the ultimate
Door

No, he may not be the one for you

But after meeting you

He should be encouraged to

Seek the Lord until he finds his very own love so true

And you would be

Able to see

How your kindness to him

Helped him to find his very own good thing

No Sis, he may not be your chosen One but He is still certainly God's chosen Son

What are considerate ways to let a gentleman know that you are not interested in him?

Kingdom Woman

"Who knows? Maybe you were made queen for just such a time as this."?"
Esther 4:14b

My feet move at the sound of His voice
As He directs my mouth speaks. - I am a Kingdom Woman

I am filled with His fruits
His Spirit overflows within me – I am a Kingdom Woman

My bank accounts are filled with great treasure
I have provision and grace without measure
I am a Kingdom Woman

I have no need to fear or worry about future times
God takes care of all of my needs as I keep first Him on my mind
I am a Kingdom Woman

Worldly men and suitors out there mean nothing to me
If they cannot see like I see
God's vision, purpose, plan and destiny for me
I am a Kingdom Woman

Yes, I have ambition and desires but I know it's not all about me

It's all about the King of Kings and His purposes within me

I am a Kingdom Woman

I employ my gifts and talents so to bless the world

And make no mistake about it I'm Holy Spirit led and guided, I stand on God's word

I am a Kingdom Woman

I dress for success because I am blessed

It's not to gain attention; I can't help it if you're impressed

I am a Kingdom Woman

I give to the poor and help them to see

That God can give them witty inventions and ideas just like He gave them me

I am a Kingdom Woman

I operate with an excellent spirit in my companies

I keep in mind my friends and those who accompany me

I am a Kingdom Woman

My words give life to all who come to me

But they also speak death to the plans of the enemy

I am a Kingdom Woman

I decree and declare wealth

I speak and proclaim health
I am a Kingdom Woman

I am honored to be a woman
So I wear my crown well
I am a kingdom woman

I encourage the men of Valor
To acknowledge the Kingship of God in them
I am a Kingdom Woman

I train my children, I keep my home and I protect
I treat my husband with honor, courtesy and the utmost
respect
I am a Kingdom Woman

I am here on earth on assignment temporarily
I will be all that God has sent me to be
A missionary, an emissary
I am a Kingdom Woman

Daily I am disciplined
I listen to Him
That's why ….
I am a Kingdom Woman

How can a Kingdom woman honor God in her daily life?

The Reason

"I consider that our present sufferings are not worth comparing with the glory that will be revealed in us" Romans 8:18

Choose to wait because I know that you are worth it

God never short changes those who truly trust in HIM

I am going to wait because I know I deserve it

I will reap what I sow and in the end I know I will win

More than a Good man, a Godly man, a great man

A High priest, a King ready to lead

This is what I have been waiting for all of these years

For this I have been sowing in prayers, fasting, service and with tears

Because I refuse to not allow God to prove His goodness to me

In the midst of a generation who may laugh, mock, scorn and ridicule me

I take a stand to delay my desire for frivolous attention

And with my will, submit to God every longing of the soul for inopportune affection

Knowing that good things come to those that are patient and still

And until, my change has come,

I will marinate in this process, while in preparation, knowing that I will

Be ready for you when you come to me

A man with a spirit of excellence like Joseph

And a heart of humility like Uriah

A heart of worship like King David

The Wisdom of Solomon and the purity of King Josiah

A man who like the Apostle Peter, possesses boldness and humility

Doing the work of the ministry while caring for his family

Like the Apostle Paul persistent in life fulfilling the call

And like the Prince of Peace Jesus Christ

Willing to offer his very life for his bride, His all in all

Yes, I am waiting for a mighty man of valor- skilled with the Word of God

Who can catch me if I fall

Gently correct me when I'm wrong

Encourage me when I'm right

Be my best friend all my life

This is Reason enough to be strong

Reason enough to hold on

Reason enough to be wise

The reason to not compromise

Therefore, I say

Choose to wait because I know that You are worth it

God never short changes those who truly trust in HIM

I am going to wait because I know I deserve it

I will reap what I sow and in the end I know I will win

What is your reason?

The Proverbs 31 Man

"Her husband is greatly respected when he deliberates with the city fathers."
Proverbs 31:23

He leads his family in the things of God
He is a vital contributor on his job
He keeps a record of all he earns
He gives continuously to the House of the Lord

He is faithful to his beautiful wife
He knows her very well because he has invested in to her life
He has given his all to see her blossom and be
His precious beautiful bride
and all that God desires for her to be

He has prepared and made provision for his sons
He trains them for life while they are young
His olive branches around his table and arrows in his hand
He will release them to dominate and increase in this land

He is dressed with the best robes, the robes of a king
He has swagger in in his step
because He knows it's a God thing
He extends his arms to help anyone He may see
He opens his heart to the troubled and down trodden when
they are in need

31

He is well known for his kindness in the community

He handles all of his enterprises and businesses with honesty
and integrity

He blesses his parents and parent's parents like good sons
always do

He teaches his children and children's children to honor them
too

He prays with faith, humility, and strength

He ushers his family into God's very presence

He leads them in holiness

He is the Virtuous Man, the man of strength, honor, character
and faith

His wife and children can trust in him and know it will be all
OK

"Many men do great things, but you excel them all"

Good looks may fade

like the paint on a shiny black Mercedes Benz

But a man with a heart after God should be praised

Cause in the Lord alone He trusts and obeys

Yes, Good looks may fade, but the man with a heart after God
will always be remembered, honored and praised.

Are there any men in your community who have shown the character of a Proverbs 31 man?

I Am Beautiful

"I thank you, High God - you're breathtaking! Body and soul, I am marvelously made! I worship in adoration - what a creation!" Psalm 139:14

I am one of the most beautiful women on the face of the planet…. can't you see?

The beauty of the Most High God Himself is radiating and shinning right through me!

From the crown of my head to the soles of my feet…

I am 100% handcrafted, creatively designed, I am unique!

And oh no, no, no, no, if you are around me you don't need to feel insecure

Cause, Yes, the Lord is mine but He also can be yours

Everything He touches turns to instant beauty

Heaven comes to earth through His children who do His duty

No need for an attitude when I have all these fruits!

With a soft answer and wisdom from above I can influence you

to do -what you are supposed to!

Though there is a lot in this package, it's sealed…cause it ain't free

I been Redeemed…someone has paid the price for me!!!

There you have it

I am beautiful inside and it is shining out

Simply because God says it...

I am fearfully and wonderfully made...

there is absolutely no doubt!

In what ways is God's beauty displayed through your life?

His Love

*"I've never quit loving you and never will.
Expect love, love, and more love!" Jeremiah 31:3*

I thank God so much

for His love.

It is unfailing; it is consistent-real love

It is pure; it's persistent-true love

It is unfeigned; it is unconditional-Good love

It's forever, eternal- His love

More than religious, Not just traditional-real love

It's life giving, it's strengthening-true love

It's reviving, it's refreshing-good love

it's Oh so beautiful- His love!

It takes the ugly things and makes them glorious

it takes the broken, down cast and defeated and makes them victorious

it takes the fearful and makes them bold,

it can take the foolish and makes them wise like the old.

It takes rubbish and transform it in to gold

it breathes new life and vision to the worn and weary soul

It takes the orphan, the unloved and gives him identity

How I thank my Father,

How I thank the Son, the Lord Jesus Christ

How thank the precious Holy Spirit
for the love that has been granted unto me!
I am ever grateful for this unfailing love
Unending, transcending-His love
Always shielding, always protecting -real love
Constantly wooing, continually correcting-true love
Endlessly covering, faithfully reaching -good love
Evermore true showing me- that unconditionally- He has given me-
His love

Good love, real love, true love
Forever I will be experiencing everlasting
love with Him above!

How often do you get to sit and truly meditate on the fact that God's love for you will last for eternity and it is unconditional?

It takes time

"But I trust in you, LORD;
I say, "You are my God." My times are in your hands;
deliver me from the hands of my enemies,
from those who pursue me.," Psalm 31:14-15 (NIV)

Sometimes it takes years

for God to heal

wounds within us so deep

It takes nights

of Him ministering

to us in our sleep.

Allowing His word

to wash away fears

and so many lies

So many moments

of staring deeply into His eyes

His truth assures us that we are loved,

His undefiled, beloved
and at anytime

welcomed

to come

humbly

to His throne

as His precious, His very own

I have learned to dance
in the palm of His hands
And understand
His love
as He whispers softly to me His plans
Plans to prosper me
good thoughts of me
amazingly filling are His words of peace
overflowing with hope, future and destiny
And it takes time
Yes, it takes time
Cause it takes time
to renew the mind
Time to meditate, meditate
rehearse and rehearse
medicate and medicate
that heart with His words
Daily remembering what He says-those words can't get lost
keep them in your heart; keep them in your head
Cause they rid of self-destructive self-annihilating thoughts
And they don't remind you of what you have not
They remind you of Who He is in you and what it is you've got
New life in Him so sweet
Rivers of joy overflowing
peace of mind so free

reaping and sowing

breakthrough and deliverance (yes, the chains, they all break)

supernatural strength

Christ-in-You the Hope of glory-give Him praise!

Godly confidence

and

though He fills and enters you as soon as you ask

Time may pass

as you learn to hold fast

to His promises

what He says

Yes, it truly takes time

to be refined

as He has designed

you to be

But He is the Lord of Time- Selah!

Enjoy the Journey,

And you will be fine!

And in time

Have that renewed heart and mind

And be able to say with full assurance

All His promises are mine!

What are some of the benefits that you have experienced from spending time in God's presence?

<u>Hold on to HIS Hands</u>

"That's why we can be so sure that every detail in our lives of love for God is worked into something good." Romans 8:28

I don't understand

Everything

but this makes me want to

hold on to the HANDS

of the MAN

with the PLAN

stronger, tighter, firmer and longer than ever before.

He says that we must simply trust Him in

Everything and

allow Him

to move

hold on to His HANDS

cause He's the MAN

with the PLAN

He's greater, bigger; better, more powerful than any other.

Praise Him in the midst of

everything

give Him glory, and thank Him...know

He is there holding you with His HANDS
he is the MAN

with the PLAN

You will never be put to shame if you do this cause he makes

everything

work for the good of those who love Him

so trust harder, more confidently, more delightfully

Because

He is the MAN

with the PLAN

Hold on to HIS HANDS

If you truly embrace the truth that you don't have to figure out life on your own and that God has the master plan, do you think that you should ever be worried?

No more disappointments

*"Never walk away from Wisdom—she guards your life;
love her—she keeps her eye on you.
Above all and before all, do this: Get Wisdom!
Write this at the top of your list: Get Understanding!" Proverbs 4:6&7*

Whenever you self-appoint
It's likely that you will be dis appointed
Cause who appointed you there in the first place?

Promotion comes from God
not just on your job
But I am talking about looking for a soul mate

I know you thought He was cute
But apparently all the other women think he is too
Even though you were 100% sure
He was looking directly at you

And when it was time to greet at church
His eyes "locked" with yours
And you were so sure this was the "one"
That you went home and told all the girls

You batted your eyes and
Sent your prayers up
"Lord if He is for me,
Please let us meet up"

You fixed your hair and your nails
put on Your Sunday best dress suit
You gave God a crazy praise saying
"Lord I just know, this is You"

But the brother in the Lord still has yet to say hello
You haven't even met him yet 'because he is always on the go
And Sis, your heart is too precious to just give it to someone you
don't even know
Heart break is around the corner he is not even your friend, how

Worth the Wait

could he be a Beau?

Then two weeks later after church
you walk to the parking lot where you first locked eyes
There he is hugged up with his kids and his beautiful wife to your
surprise
Now you have to hold back the cries

You wave in awe
And smile with total dismay
"Lord, I thought he was the one for me"

You are not the only one to experience this, my dear
Trust me it's true
It has happened to the best of them
men and women too

Don't appoint yourself and you won't be disappointed
Just like you can't call yourself to do anything you
must be graced you must be anointed
When God is hooking you up, my friend, you will surely know
And you won't have to strive and cry because it will just flow

He will surely lead by His word and His voice
Choosing a mate is still a choice
He leads and will advise
Trust Him as you choose wisely to see through His eyes

And know that you are a precious jewel
Far above rubies, like a royal crown set in a case
And when He presents that special someone to you
He will introduce you face to face

God is not a God of confusion
He is a God of order
He knows exactly how to bless His people
His blessings always make rich and add no sorrow

What God joins together no man can place apart
Until the Lord releases you guard and protect your heart
Don't self-appoint, let God bring your increase

45

You won't be disappointed
You will be so blessed that God's faithfulness
Everyone will be able to see!

Do you understand the importance of guarding your heart with all diligence and wisdom?

Single but not alone

"Be strong. Take courage. Don't be intimidated. Don't give them a second thought because GOD, your God, is striding ahead of you. He's right there with you. He won't let you down; he won't leave you." Deuteronomy 31:6

S.......so every one is saying you should wait
I-think I have waited long enough
N- No I haven't met the right one yet
G-give me a break I am doing my best
L-Love is what I am waiting for
E- Everyone else seems to be walking through that door

B- But I am learning that I am a unique person all by myself
U- Understanding that I am blessed
T- Taking on the armor of God and daily getting dressed

N-Nightly embracing the presence of God and becoming
O- Overjoyed with His presence that He reveals to me
T- Taking seriously the Gospel story of Romance that He wrote to me

A- Always abounding in the work of the Lord
L= Letting go of all that seeks to make life null & void
O= Offering myself daily as a sacrifice in spirit & in truth
N= Now I know what spending time with God can do
E- Empty no...But filled, yes! Because I am single eyed my Lord in YOU!!

C= Complete in Christ, totally secure
O= Opened heavens and open doors
M=Mountain moving faith
P= Passionate praise
L= Letting go of all fears
E= Echoing the song of the Lord as I hear it
T= Taking my rightful place as His daughter
E= Expressing the real heart of the Father

I= Intimate with the Holy Spirit
N= No one can break up our relationship or interfere with it

C= Cause I am complete in Christ
H=He is my confidence
R= Reassuring me of His love for me minute by minute
I= I simply cannot move, live, breath or have my being
without Him
S= So I am single but definitely not alone
T=The Lord is not just with me, He is in me and has made my
heart his home

I AM SINGLE BUT NOT ALONE!

*Did you know that the definition of single
means "only one" not "lonely"?*

<u>You are the One</u>

"But now, this is what the LORD says— he who created you, Jacob, he who formed you, Israel: "Do not fear, for I have redeemed you; I have summoned you by name; you are mine." Isaiah 43:1 (NIV)

You are the One who loves me more than anyone ever could
You are the One who loves me more than anyone ever would
When my heart and emotions are pressured by the stresses of life
You console me
Lord you hold me

You are the One who cares like nobody else would dare
You are the One who embraces and comforts
You are the One who is always there
You shield me
You are here with me

You help me to display beauty in all that I do
You help me to renew my thinking
You help me to be more like You
You don't blame me
You train me

You are the best thing that has ever happened in my life
You make me smile every morning and
You give me sweet sleep at night
You cover me
You hover over me

You are the One the only One I know
You are the One the One who loves me so
You are the Shield that blocks every attack
You are in front of me, beside me and behind me
You have got my back

You are the One, number one, not number two
You are the source of my confidence Precious One it's you
You are the reason that I have any strength to live
You are the One whose passion enables me to give
There is no more searching

You are my friend
always encouraging
never discouraging
ever uplifting
never belittling
faith speaking
constantly believing
You are *"numero uno"*
"Numero un"
In every language
You are number one
You are the One!

***Who in this world can love you more than the One who created
you?***

Mary, Mary, Merry

"But I, yes I, am the one who takes care of your sins—that's what I do. I don't keep a list of your sins." Isaiah 43:25

If your story didn't start out so great
who's to say it can't end well
you may be like the virgin Mary
You may be like the woman at the well

You may have been chaste
knowing no man
You may have given away your heart too many times
to count on your hand

but the same God that saves one-is the same God who saves
all
and no one can say that they are good on their own-no one at
all

Because all He asks is obedience and faith
From this moment on just simply choose to obey
Isn't he the God that makes bitter waters sweet?
And from the adulterous relationship
allowed the birth of the richest and wisest king

Sure if you know better do better-because consequences are
great
the pain of sin can be devastating- the pain of sin brings
feelings of shame, confusion and hate

But if you have changed your mind
And repented from the wrong
Believe the Lord is able
to turn it all around

He is a good, good God-The Father, Our Father, Father God

He is a good, good, God
So whether Mary the mother of Jesus
Or whether Mary Magdalene
God will make your story end beautifully
If you only surrender you heart of hearts to HIM
Mary or Mary it can all end merry

Regardless of your story, did you know that if you surrender
your heart to Christ, he can still get the glory?

Rejoice in Testing

*"Anyone who meets a testing challenge head-on and manages to stick it
out is mighty fortunate. For such persons loyally in love with God, the
reward is life and more life."*
James 1:12

So refreshing
when you pass the testings
life brings them daily
no matter who you are

It's such a blessing-to know God is at the ending
of those trials-trust in Him, He won't let you fall

Because when it seems like you're failing
know your faith is yet prevailing
If you have been standing on
His Victorious Word

Cause it's more than your feelings-It's all about His dealings
He backs up and performs His unfailing, glorious Word

In the face of the trials-Don't be in denial
Simply choose to obey what He says

Be diligent with it-You're going win it
Know He has heard all of your prayers

Laugh your socks off-Turn the phone off
Dance and Praise-for the battle is won

Rejoice again and again
The Lords joy is your strength
Worship Him, Because before you asked
the breakthrough has already come!

Do you find joy in trials knowing that you will receive a reward for overcoming them through Christ?

So is the Man that Findeth

*"Find a good spouse, you find a good life—
and even more: the favor of GOD!" Proverbs 18:22*

You are such a good thing sent from God above

Being prepared for that man of God who will shower you with

unconditional love

Never settle for less than what God desires

He sacrificed himself for his bride; a man who will give all is

what is required

He must be able to see you as His favor

If He is not the right one then he will only see you as labor

More work, more responsibility, another mouth to feed

I don't have time for this I need to take care of my own wants

and needs

But if He is a good match sent from Jehovah Jireh

He is prepared to be that leader for you, thrilled for the

opportunity to be a provider

A priest of His home ready to fill the mouth of his seed with

words of life

Ever thankful to God for giving him such a prudent and

excellent wife

Knowing he has been rewarded because the Lord has placed

you upon him like a Crown

His smile is from ear to ear.....trust me He will be cheesing like

a clown

He will say "you are so virtuous worth more than diamonds,

rubies, or any pearl

and you are a true crown to my life-Woman you have brought

favor into my world"

Do you see yourself as the "treasure" and "favor" that God says that you are?

I didn't know

"If we claim that we're free of sin, we're only fooling ourselves. A claim like that is errant nonsense. On the other hand, if we admit our sins—make a clean breast of them—he won't let us down; he'll be true to himself. He'll forgive our sins and purge us of all wrongdoing"
I John: 1:8-9

I didn't know

Some things I just didn't know

I had to figure them out all on my own

Please believe me when I say

I hate the school of hard knocks

A simple youth trying to navigate

Not realizing that whatever I see is what I attempted to

emulate

Brick walls-Roll calls

Sleepless nights-Bloody fights

I didn't know, I really didn't know

Fairy tales-Mind games

Broken glasses-Time passes

I didn't know I really didn't know

But not knowing is not a valid excuse

Because now I have a manual for life

The Good book shows all of humanity how not- to-lose

Or misuse

The precious life and time

God has given to you

If you admit you really didn't know

Keep in mind -there is still hope

The first step to recovering

Is to admit that-There is a problem with

the way that you have been doing things

Now it's time to know

precious promises so true

Loving kindness daily new

Wise words so pure

Courage to endure

Now it's time to know

How to take the right steps

Allow God to clean up every mess

Excellently passing every test

Strength, power, and rest

Now you can know

And now you know that you know

That you don't have to not know

Because wisdom and knowledge is here

Crying out to give you the wisdom that you need to succeed

Why be condemned by your past mistakes when God has an amazing future in mind for your life in Him through His wisdom and understanding?

Boyfriend and Girlfriend

"There are "friends" who destroy each other, but a real friend sticks closer than a brother" Proverbs 18:24 NLT

Boyfriend and Girlfriend
A true friend or a dead end

A confidant or a villain
A blessing or a cursing

Encourager or Setback
Enhancing purity or here to distract

Pushing into purpose or pulling down the spirit
Honing my personality or adding bad things to it

Making me see the world from another positive point of view
or
Enticing me to worldliness and a lustful attitude

Inspiring to a better tomorrow,
a blessing from God, or just adding more sorrow

Speaking forth to nations or compromising to fornication
Reminding you of your worth or treating you like dirt

Cultivating or Manipulating
Fortifying or simply flesh gratifying

Opening the heart to the love of God more and more
Or sent from the enemy to steal, kill, and to destroy

So whether it be courting or dating between you and the Lord
decide
What type of person you allow into your life

Choose this day whom you will serve
The bad path of destruction or the good one that you deserve

Do you need to make changes in your relationships in this season in your life?

Knight in Shining Armor

"Then I saw Heaven open wide—and oh! A white horse and its Rider. The Rider, named Faithful and True, judges and makes war in pure righteousness. His eyes are a blaze of fire, on his head many crowns. He has a Name inscribed that's known only to himself. He is dressed in a robe soaked with blood, and he is addressed as "Word of God." Revelation 19:11-13

There is a Knight in Shining Armor

Who is on His way to me

He is called the Lord of lords

He is the King of kings

All the earth bows down before Him

Because of His glory and awe

His name is so powerful and majestic

that the sun, moon, and stars bow down

And yes He rides upon a white horse

with Sword at His side

He is patiently waiting

for His beautiful bride

Worth the Wait

I know my prince is on His way to me

I know with all that's within

It's not a fairy tale at all (it is written in the word of God)

All of it written and inspired by Him

So never feel like your dream of being a princess

won't come true

There is One called the Prince of Peace

who is recklessly, abandoned in love with you

He came from heaven to bring you close

Laid down His life as a sacrifice to pay what you owe

arose from the dead with power so that all hell would know

You mean more than life to Him...how He loves you so

There is One called Faithful and True

He is passionately

in love with You

Your Knight in shining armor He is

His word all around Him shinning-You are His

No rapper, no athlete, no man

can take his place

no friend, no job, no desire, no birthday cake

He is pure and holy

and he cares so much for you

He is your Knight in Shining armor

He is always faithful and evermore true

And remember He is coming back for you

So live with honor, integrity, courage and virtue

Stay faithful and committed

As pure, holy, spotless brides will always do

Church be ready, awaiting His return

Because He is preparing a place for you

No one knows the day nor the hour of His return

Are you preparing yourself as a bride to meet the Savior, King of kings and Lord of lords even as you prepare yourself to be an earthly bride?

The Songs

First Love

"I am Alpha and Omega, the beginning and the end, the first and the last."

Revelation 22:13

You're my first and my last my Creator

My Alpha, Omega

My Best Friend, My Savior

the first love who captured my heart

My Redeemer, My Keeper, My Lover My Leader

And I just want to walk in Your ways and do what You

want me to do

Cause I know I can't live without You

I'm living for the glory of You

I need You-You're my first love

Way before my mother's womb

You held me in Your arms and said baby I love You

And You were there on my first day of school

67

whispering softly but I couldn't hear You

In high school You caught my attention and You showed me

how much You missed me

And now I'm grown, Single not alone 'cause You've always

been here with me

So I just want to walk in Your ways and do what You want me

to do

'Cause I know I can't live without You

I'm living for the glory of You

I need You-Your my first love

I get so happy when I look in Your word

and see the letters that You've written to me

And when I look into the eyes of Your Spirit

and see You smile at me

Yet many times You're calling my name

And I act as if I don't even hear you

All you want to do is love on me, affirm me

and draw me near to You (so I'm saying)

So I just want to walk in Your ways and do what You want me

to do

'Cause I know I can't live without You

I'm living for the glory of You

I need You-You're my first love

And surely I have made some mistakes

But You've never cast me aside

You cleansed and washed, purified me and

named me as a part of Your Bride

So I just want to walk in Your ways and do what You want me

to do

'Cause I know I can't live without You-I'm living for the glory

of You

I need You-You're my first love

Father, Savior, Lover, Friend

Beginning and the End

You're the fairest of ten thousand men

Jesus, Author, Son of Man, I AM that I AM

It's a privilege to hold Your hand

So I just want to walk in Your ways and do what You want me

to do

'Cause I know I can't live without You

'Cause I know I can't live without You

I'm living for the glory of You

I need You-You're my first love

More than any other-Not a better lover

Closer than a brother-First Love

Many people say "you never get over your first love", but did you know that the truth is that God is the One who loved you first?

I'm Yours and Your Mine

"Before I shaped you in the womb,
I knew all about you. Before you saw the light of day,
I had holy plans for you: A prophet to the nations—
that's what I had in mind for you." Jeremiah 1:5

Before I was formed in my mother's womb

You knew me, You called me, You chose me

Ordained me

And every single day of my life

Was recorded before you

He who dwells in eternity He knows it all

You know when I rise and when I fall

And when I wake up You're here with me

Because I'm Yours and Your mine

I'm Yours and Your mine

Before I was formed in my mother's womb

You knew me, You called me, You chose me

Ordained me

And every single day of my life

Was recorded before you

You who dwell in eternity- You know it all

You know when I rise and when I fall

Worth the Wait

And every time I wake up-You're here with me

Because I'm Yours and Your mine
I'm Yours and Your mine

You've placed me here in the palm of Your hands
Alpha Omega You're the One fulfilling Your plans
I was born again and cleansed from my sins
All that I know is that Your love is so amazing to me
It's so amazing to me

In the midnight hour You're holding me, embracing me and
telling me that you love me
Cause I'm Yours and Your mine

*Do you realize that your entire life was seen by God before you
were even a thought in the mind of your parents?*

<u>Only in You</u>

"Say this: 'GOD, you're my refuge.
I trust in you and I'm safe!" Psalm 91:2

Only in Your loving arms I find shelter

Only in Your loving arms I find joy overflowing

In your loving arms I find shelter

Only in Your loving arms I find joy overflowing

Hold me in Your arms forever and ever I just want to be with
You

Oh Lord I give my heart to You-Surrender all I am to You

I want to live my with You-Oh Lord I give my heart to You

Only in Your loving arms I find shelter

Father, In Your loving arms I find joy overflowing

In your loving arms I find shelter

Only in Your loving arms I find joy overflowing

Hold me in Your arms forever and ever I just want to be with
You

Oh Lord I give my heart to You-Surrender all I am to You

I want to live my with You-Oh Lord I give my heart to You

I wanna walk with You, talk with You, live in You-I want to be

with You

I wanna walk with You, talk with You, live in You-I want to be
with You

Hold me in Your arms forever Lord

*Is there anywhere else besides the presence of God where you
can truly have and feel complete safety?*

<u>True Love</u>

"Many waters cannot quench love, neither can the floods drown it: if a man would give all the substance of his house for love, it would utterly be contemned."
Song of Songs8:7 (KJV)

True Love is hard to find

Many search a life time

Wondering how to feel its embrace

But true Love rests in the Father's face

Many waters can not quench His love no flood no flood can drown it away

Many waters cannot quench His love

No One No one can take it away

Many waters cannot quench His love no flood no flood can drown it away

Many waters cannot quench His love

His love is unconditional

Tearful nights

Yes, I have cried

But You have washed them from my eyes

With unconditional

The Father's love, agape love, You have given to me

It's unchangeable

Worth the Wait

You call me Yours, give me Your love

Who can take it from me nobody

Many waters cannot quench His love no flood no flood can drown it away

Many waters cannot quench His love

No One No one can take it away

Many waters cannot quench His love no flood no flood can drown it away

Many waters cannot quench His love

His love is unconditional

Ablazed and burning

My heart is yearning for you Dove, my True Love

You light my fire

My One desire is to know You

So that I can serve You

What can separate me from the love of God which is in Christ Jesus that You've given to me?

What can separate me from the love of God which is in Christ Jesus than He's given to me?

WHO can separate me from the Love of God no, no, no, nothing!

No death

No life

Nothing present

Nothing to come

No principality no nothing

Nobody

Nobody

What is the definition of True Love?

Delight in You

"Jesus answered and said to him, 'If anyone loves me, he will keep My word; and My Father will love him, and We will come to him and make Our home with him." John 14:23 (NIV)

In Your presence there's fullness of joy- at Your right hand pleasures ever more

so many blessings that you have in store for your people

SO we lift up our heads to the sky-in Your presence we seek to abide

Oh yes how we delight Jehovah

Ooooh, we delight in You

For we know that the whole earth Yours-Everything and the fullness thereof

Set our hearts on things up above- We're Your people

Seek to please You in all that we do

Here we are to worship You

Oh Yes how we delight in You Jehovah

Ooooh, we delight in You

He'll do it He'll do it yes He'll do it

Now..If I abide in You and You abide in me I can ask what I will- it will be given to me

So let your word abide-Let Your word abide in me

If I live in You, and You live in me,

I can ask what I will- it will be given to me

How has finding delight in Christ rather than in the temporary things of this world changed your life?

Living Sacrifice

"Therefore, I urge you, brothers and sisters, in view of God's mercy, to offer your bodies as a living sacrifice, holy and pleasing to God—this is our true and proper worship." Romans 12:1

It's the least that I can do

Giving my body to You

It's the least that I can do

Giving my soul to You

The least that I can do

Giving my mind to You

You've died and rose for me

So I must freely

Offer my body to You

Holy, Acceptable in Your eyes

Pleasing in Your sight

A Living Sacrifice

You've done so much for me

You've given me what I need

You held me up in the darkest hours of my life

When no one else was around

You never let me down

I see why they say

You're Closer than a brother

Cause You're always by my side

I can't go nowhere without You here with me
I can't go anywhere, You're my liberty
I want to thank You for everything You've done
I want to show You
Holy One, You're the Only One

It's the least that I can do
Giving my body to You
It's the least that I can do
Giving my soul to You
The least that I can do
Giving my mind to You
You've died and rose for me
So I must freely
Offer my body to You
Holy, Acceptable in Your eyes
Pleasing in Your sight
A Living Sacrifice

You're always watching me
Eternally
You foreknew me
Your heart, Your promise

You died and rose to set me free

Now death has lost its sting

I can't go nowhere without You here with me

I can't go anywhere, You're my liberty

I want to thank You for everything You've done

I want to show You

Holy One, You're the Only One

When you think of how much Christ has sacrificed to provide you with eternal life, is it too much for Him to ask that you love him wholeheartedly?

<u>Holy Yours</u>

"But now thus says the Lord, he who created you, O Jacob, he who formed you, O Israel: "Fear not, for I have redeemed you; I have called you by name, you are mine". Isa 43:1 ESV

You're my passion

Everlasting

Show me how to

serve You Lord

I feel You near me

Your voice so clearly

Teach me how to

love You Lord

I'm holy Yours, only Yours

Only Yours- holy, only

Holy Yours, Only Yours

Only Yours- holy only yours

Captivated

By Your presence

Keep me in Your

Perfect will

My heart is Yours, Lord

Only Yours Lord

Worth the Wait

Do with it just
As You will

I'm holy Yours, only Yours
Only Yours- holy, only
Holy Yours, Only Yours
Only Yours- holy only yours

Cause I belong to You
Yes I do
Cause I belong to You
Yes its true
Cause I belong to You, Jesus

*Do you consider it as an honor to give your life back to the one
who paid the price and gave His life for you?*

Devoted to You

"because it is written, "You shall be holy (set apart), for I am holy."
I Peter 1:16 AMP

My soul's desire
My hearts on fire
Cause I'm inspired
Ready to do Your will
You are my passion
Love everlasting
That's why I'm asking
Help me to do Your will

I want to be wholly yours
I want to be only Yours
Righteousness, holy Yours
Holy, Only, Righteous, Holy
Devoted (Belonging) to You

For You I'm Living
My all I'm giving
Be thou my vision
I'm gonna do Your will
My life's submitted

Fully committed
Cause Lord (Not me) You did it
Now I've got to do Your will

I want to be wholly yours
I want to be only Yours
Righteousness, Only Yours
Holy, Only, Righteous, Holy
Devoted (Belonging) to You

Wholly, Only, Holy, Righteous, Holy

*Why do you think that God commands His children to be holy,
devoted and separated for Him?*

Purity is Power

"Therefore, if anyone cleanses himself from these *things* [which are dishonorable—disobedient, sinful], he will be a vessel for honor, sanctified [set apart for a special purpose and], useful to the Master, prepared for every good work."2 Tim2:21 AMP

I lift my hands up to the sky

I life my hands up way up high

All praises to You my King; You're the Ruler of my Life

Cause I know it's to you I belong

And that is why I sing this song

Cause Your heart is always searching for the heart that's searching for you

Purity is power

I use my lips to bless my neighbor

I use my hands to help my brother

All praises to You my God; You said to love one another

Cause I know it's to you I belong

And that is why I sing this song

Cause Your heart is always searching for the heart that's searching for you

Said Your heart is always searching for the heart that's searching for you

Purity is power

It's strength in the midnight hour
Its joy in the good and the bad
Its peace when everything's crazy
It's giving love when you should be mad

Purity is power

Its proof that our God is living
Its evidence Jesus is alive
It's His Holy Spirit working inside me
That causes me to walk upright

Purity is power

It's putting on all of Your armor
Its keeping Jesus Christ on my mind
It's the grace to heal the sick
Its recovering of sight to the blind

Purity is power

When you live for Him
You sanctify Your life to Him
You know it pleases Him
When you live Your life for Him

You live in purity
sanctify your life to Him
You give Him everything
when you live your life for Him

You know He wants You to
sanctify your life to Him
You know that this is true
When you live your life for Him

He'll be your everything
sanctify Your life to Him
He'll give You all You need
When You live Your life for Him

Purity is power

What are some things that God is challenging you to let go of so that you can be a Holy Vessel of Honor?

Content

"But those who wait upon God get fresh strength. They spread their wings and soar like eagles, They run and don't get tired, they walk and don't lag behind"

Isaiah 40:31

Lord I'm content to wait

because in waiting I find patience they that wait upon the Lord
they renew their strength

Lord I'm content to wait

because in waiting I find patience they that wait upon the Lord
they renew their strength

Here I am one again

Believing what You said in Your word about me

I ain't got no reasons to give up

Cause I know Your word is working in me

Don't need no reasons why, don't even need to try to figure it
out

Your God and I'm not

So I come humbly

I bow down on my knees

Your faithful and true

So I'm waiting on You

Worth the Wait

Lord I'm content to wait

because in waiting I find patience they that wait upon the Lord
shall renew their strength

Lord I'm content to wait

because in waiting I find patience they that wait upon the Lord
shall renew their strength

While I'm waiting, I'm anticipating

Cause I know Your word is working in me

Not gone change what I've been saying this whole time

Cause You said if I believed then it is mine

As I abide and hide Your Holy word inside

'Til I say that You Oh Lord fulfills my hearts desires

Your Kingdom Come in me

Your will be done in me

Your faithful and true

So I'm waiting on You

Wait on the Lord

I'm spending time with you

Wait on the Lord

I do what You say to do

Wait on the Lord

Know that the Lord is coming through

Wait on the Lord

He's gonna do what He said He'd do

Why don't you

Wait, wait, wait, wait, wait

Wait, Wait, Wait, Wait the Lord

Don't You know He'll do it- Yeah

Wait, wait, wait, wait, wait

Wait, Wait, Wait, Wait the Lord

Can you pinpoint any situation in life where you were so glad that you waited?

The Only One

"I, yes I, am GOD.
I'm the only Savior there is." Isaiah 43:11

I only want to be with You
I want to be together
Only in Your loving arms Lord
Always and forever
I only want to seek Your Face
So You will be beside me
Lord I only want to be with You

The Only One
You are the One my soul desires
The Only One
You are the One my heart beats for
The Only One
You are the One my soul desires
The Only One
You are the One
You are the One

Said I only want to be with You
I love to be together
Walking with you daily Oh God
Soon it will be forever
I'm grateful that You sent Your Son
And now You live inside me
Lord I only want to be with You

The Only One
You are the One my soul desires
The Only One
You are the One my heart beats for
The Only One

You are the One my soul desires
The Only One
You are the One
You are the One

*Why search for another when you know there is only One
Savior?*

Seek Your Face

"When my heart whispered, "Seek God," my whole being replied,
"I'm seeking him!" Psalm 27:8

I'll seek your face
for all my days
I'll follow You
In all my ways
I'll press into
the Holy Place
Oh God I want to
live in Your embrace

Oh God,
Oh Jesus Christ
Oh Master, Master, Your worthy)
I'll keep seeking Your Face

I love You
I worship You
With my heart my all
even to my knees I fall
I cry out to you
I give to You

Much more than die for you
Lord I live for you

Oh God, Oh Jesus Christ
Oh Master, Master, Your worthy)
I'll keep seeking Your Face

In Spirit and Truth
Promise to honor You
In all I do
Want to be Just like You
Faithful and True

You are God, Your Eternal, You're Holy
You are God; You're Eternal, Your Holy
I lift my Hands and I praise You cause Your worthy
I lift my hands and I praise You cause Your worthy

How does your life reflect your pursuit and passion for God? Do you seek His Face?

Can you feel Him?

"But a time is coming and is already here when the true worshipers will worship the Father in spirit [from the heart, the inner self] and in truth; for the Father seeks such people to be His worshipers." John 4:23 AMP

Can You feel Him? Can You feel Him in the atmosphere?

The presence of the Holy God is here

He is healing, He is moving, He is setting free

He is Jesus let us worship His majesty

That's why we worship Jesus

Come and worship Jesus

Worship Jesus

I can feel You. I can feel You in the atmosphere

Your presence Oh Holy God You're here

You have healed me

You've delivered me

You have set me free

My Jesus, I worship Your majesty

That's why I worship You Jesus

Come on and worship Jesus
Worship Jesus

You're real, You're real, You're real, You're real

You're real, You're real, You're real, You're real

I can feel You

I hear You

I see You

I feel You

I can feel You

I hear You

I see You

I feel You

I praise You

I love You

Adore You

I praise You

I worship

Exalt You

Magnify You Jesus

Lift Your Name

Exalt You

Magnify You Jesus

Can You feel Him? Can You feel Him in the atmosphere?

The presence of the Holy God is here
He is healing, He is moving, He is setting free
He is Jesus let us worship His majesty

Do you realize that God is listening and waiting to hear your heart and ready to answer you with His Holy word?

Final Words

&

Prayer of Salvation

My prayer for you is that...

these poems and songs have encouraged your heart. No one is saying that it is easy to walk in purity and to be abstinent until marriage, but with the strength of God, it is possible. I want to encourage you that no matter where you are in your journey to continue to follow Christ and His ways. He will always lead you in the right direction- the right direction to your purpose, the right direction to your destiny, the right direction to His love, the right direction that points always to Him as the center of your life. If you have been honoring God in your singleness, I urge you to and pray that you continue to honor Him in it. If you have fallen, I pray that you be strengthened; get back up and keep moving forward. You can do all things through Christ who strengthens you and He is able to keep you from falling and to present you blameless (Jude 1:24). Remember in this life's journey whatever you do unto the Lord will be honored by Him and in time you will be able to see that it was all Worth the Wait!

If you have read this book but you do not know God... *as your Father, your Friend and Love or at one time you were close to Him, but you walked away from His ways- now is the best time for you to come back to Him because He is the One who loves you more than any other! The Bible teaches that everyone has sinned and fallen short of God's glory (Romans 3:23). We all need a Savior. We all need Him. The Bible also says that the way that we receive forgiveness for our sins is by simply asking God to forgive us (Romans 10:9-10). The best part about asking for His forgiveness is that we can also begin a relationship with Him, a true friendship with the King of the Universe.*

Please say this prayer for salvation:

"Dear God,
I believe in You. I believe that You are real and I want to know You. I admit that I am a sinner and that I need forgiveness that only you can provide. I believe that Your Son Jesus Christ died on the cross for my sins and rose from the dead for my forgiveness from sin. I ask you Lord to come into my heart. I give my life to you. Fill me with Your Precious Holy Spirit. Help me to understand You as I read Your Word. Show me your ways Lord and I will follow. I receive your love and Your Spirit right now. In the name of Jesus Christ, I pray. Amen.

If you just prayed that prayer...

for the first time or as a recommitment to God, I am overjoyed and overflowing with happiness for you because I know that God is going to show up in a mighty way in your life! If you are not joined to a local church, I pray that God will lead you to a church where you can grow in your relationship with Him and in Your Christian walk.

If you enjoyed Worth the Wait *and you would like to keep up with* Sherice Lanae *for information on new books and upcoming events please visit* www.shericelanae.com. *You can also follow her on social media:*
Instagram, Facebook, YouTube *and* Twitter:
@shericelanae

Worth the Wait

Made in the USA
Columbia, SC
09 July 2018